MASTERING THE ART OF BECOMING A HIGH-VALUE MALE

ROCKY SAGGOO

To all the men who dare to dream, who strive for greatness, and who refuse to settle for mediocrity: this book is dedicated to you.

May you find within these pages the inspiration, guidance, and wisdom to unlock your true potential and become the high-value male you were always meant to be.

May you embrace your individuality, cultivate your strengths, and stand tall in the face of adversity.

May you reject the limitations imposed by society and forge your own path with courage, integrity, and authenticity.

May you never lose sight of your worth, your power, and your capacity to make a positive impact in the world.

This book is dedicated to the men who dare to believe in themselves and in the limitless possibilities that await them.

Here's to becoming the best version of yourself – for yourself, and for the world.

Contents

Foreword   *vii*

Preface   *ix*

1. Unleashing Your Inner Alpha   1

2. Understanding High-Value Masculinity   4

3. Building Confidence And Self-Assurance   8

4. Cultivating Leadership Skills   14

5. Mastering Communication And Influence   20

6. Honing Emotional Intelligence   26

7. Setting Goals And Achieving Success   31

8. Strengthening Relationships And Connections   37

9. Fitness, Health, And Wellness Strategies   42

10. Overcoming Challenges And Adversity   48

11. Polishing The Diamond - Mastering Personality Grooming   52

12. From Ordinary To Extraordinary: Lessons From Five Books On   63
High-Value Living

Foreword

Welcome to Mastering the Art of Becoming a High-Value Male. In this no-nonsense and gritty guide, get ready to jump on a kick-ass journey of self-discovery and transformation. Whether you're out to crush it in your personal relationships, dominate in your professional life, or simply become the ultimate version of yourself, this book serves up raw truths and badass strategies to help you conquer your goals.

In today's rapidly changing world, the concept of what it means to be a "high-value male" can often feel like a moving target. With societal norms flipping and expectations evolving, it's easy to feel lost or unsure about how to boss up in the modern world of manhood. That's where High- value male steps in.

Backed by a truckload of research, real-world experiences, and rock-solid principles, this book lays down a no-holds-barred roadmap for those who hunger to embody the qualities of a high-value male. From mastering the art of fearless communication to cultivating an irresistible presence, each chapter is a power-packed arsenal designed to arm you with the knowledge and skills to own any social or romantic scene.

But Mastering the Art of Becoming a High-Value Male isn't just about snagging attention or scoring with the ladies. It's about embracing your true self, cultivating self-respect, and forging powerful connections with others. By shining a light on the importance of self-improvement and personal growth, this book empowers you to flip societal stereotypes and redefine success on your own terms.

As you dive headfirst into this life-altering journey, I dare you to tackle each chapter with a hunger for change and a killer instinct. Whether you're a seasoned pro or just starting out on your path to self-improvement, there's something here for everyone. So, buckle up and let's raid the treasure trove of secrets to becoming the most desirable male in any room.

Preface

In a world where the dynamics of attraction and influence are constantly evolving, mastering the art of becoming a high-value male has never been more crucial. Welcome to the community of High-Value Male, where we delve deep into the principles and practices that empower men to rise above the ordinary and become the most desirable individuals in any room.

But what exactly does it mean to be a high-value male? Is it about wealth, physical appearance, or social status? While these factors may play a role, true high-value status transcends superficial attributes. At its core, it's about embodying qualities such as confidence, authenticity, and integrity. It's about becoming the kind of person others naturally gravitate towards, respect, and admire.

In this book, we'll explore the multifaceted nature of high-value masculinity and provide you with practical strategies to cultivate these qualities within yourself. Whether you're seeking to enhance your romantic relationships, excel in your career, or simply command respect in your social circles, the principles outlined in High-value formula will serve as your guide.

But let's be clear: this journey isn't about becoming someone you're not. It's about unlocking your full potential and embracing the best version of yourself. It's about recognizing your strengths, addressing your weaknesses, and striving for continuous growth and improvement.

Throughout these pages, you'll discover insights gleaned from psychology, sociology, and personal development, as well as real-life anecdotes and actionable advice from individuals who have successfully navigated their own paths to high-value status. Whether you're a seasoned veteran or just beginning your journey of self-discovery, there's something here for everyone.

So, if you are prepared to commence a transformative journey towards realizing your full potential as a desirable man, I welcome you to accompany me as we delve into the principles of High- Value Male. Together, we will unlock the traits that define your true potential.

CHAPTER ONE

Unleashing Your Inner Alpha

This is your chance to jump on a journey of self-discovery and unlock your full potential! We'll redefine what it means to be a leader in today's world. Leave behind the outdated notions of dominance and the exaggerated portrayals you've seen in movies and popular culture. Instead, we'll focus on cultivating the essential qualities of a strong leader: unwavering confidence, genuine authenticity, and the ability to inspire and motivate those around you.

Imagine commanding respect when you enter a room, not by shoutingthe loudest, but by radiating a quiet confidence that draws people in. This magnetism comes from a deep understanding of yourself, your values, and your strengths. It allows you to connect with others on a genuine level and build strong, trusting relationships. That's the kind of leadership we'restriving for.

And the best part? These qualities are already within you, waiting to be developed. Get ready to embark on this exciting adventure to tap into your inner leader and discover the powerful impact you can have on the world. You'll learn how to set a clear vision, effectively communicate your ideas, and empower others to achieve their best. As you develop these skills, you'll find yourself inspiring and motivating those around you, not through manipulation or force, but through genuine enthusiasm and a shared sense of purpose.

Welcome, gentlemen, to the genesis of your transformation. This book marks the beginning of your journey towards becoming a high-value man, an alpha in the truest sense of the word. But before we embark, let's shatter a crucial misconception: the alpha you envision from movies or hear about in locker rooms is a relic of the past. Forget the image of the domineering, chest-thumping caricature.

The modern alpha exudes a different kind of power – one rooted in leadership, confidence, and authenticity. Imagine this: you enter a room, not with boisterous pronouncements, but with a quiet strength that draws attention. People respect your presence because it embodies something genuine, something they admire. This, gentlemen, is the essence of the alpha we will cultivate together.

- ## Leadership: The Guiding Light

An alpha isn't a dictator; he's a leader. He inspires and motivates those around him. He possesses a clear vision and the charisma to unite others in pursuit of a common goal. This leadership extends beyond the boardroom or the athletic field. It's about taking initiative, being reliable, and fostering a sense of teamwork in every aspect of your life.

- ## Confidence: The Inner Compass

Confidence isn't the absence of fear; it's the ability to move forward despite it. The alpha male trusts himself, his decisions, and his ability to navigate challenges. This confidence isn't arrogance, but a quiet self-assurance that stems from self-worth and a strong foundation of personal values. As you progress through this book, you'll discover ways to build unshakeable confidence, a quality that will naturally attract others.

- ## Authenticity: The Unmasking

The most magnetic quality of any alpha is his genuineness. People are drawn to those who are comfortable in their own skin, who don't try to be someone they're not. The alpha embraces his flaws and imperfections, understanding they make him unique. This authenticity fosters trust and allows for genuine connections to be built.

- ## The Alpha Within: Unleashing Your Potential

The good news? You don't have to become someone entirely new. The alpha you seek already resides within you, waiting to be awakened. This book serves as your guide, providing the tools and strategies to unlock your leadership potential, cultivate unshakeable confidence, and embrace your authentic self. With each chapter, you'll shed layers of insecurity and self-doubt, revealing the alpha leader you were born to be.

So, gentlemen, are you ready to embark on this journey? Let's begin the transformation.

CHAPTER TWO

Understanding High-Value Masculinity

Let's toss out the outdated playbook for masculinity!

Being a man of value isn't about bulging biceps or barking orders. It's about building a foundation of unwavering integrity, the strength to overcome adversity with resilience, and the depth of character to understand and share the feelings of others (empathy). We'll climb aboard on a journey of self-discovery together, peeling back the layers to uncover the qualities that truly make a difference in today's world.

This is your invitation to a deeper understanding of yourself

We'll explore the values that shape your character and help you cultivate the traits that make you a positive force. It's time to tap into the wellspring of inner strength you possess, embrace the unique characteristics that make you who you are, and step into your power as someone who contributes meaningfully to the world around you. Imagine the impact you can have when you use your strength to lift others up, your resilience to inspire perseverance, and your empathy to build strong, supportive relationships.

Forget the dusty rulebook of outdated masculinity. Being a man of value isn't about the size of your muscles or the volume of your commands. It's about constructing a solid foundation built on *three powerful pillars:* **integrity, resilience, and empathy.**

This chapter is your guide to dismantling the old archetype and constructing a new one – the man of value. We'll toss out the tired notions of dominance and delve into the qualities that truly matter in today's world. Prepare for a journey of self-discovery, a peeling back of the layers to reveal the core characteristics that will make you a force for positive change.

This isn't about conforming to some pre-defined mold. This is an invitation to a deeper understanding of yourself. We'll explore the values that give your character its shape and help you cultivate the traits that will make you a positive influence.

Imagine the impact you can have when you:

- **Stand by your principles with unwavering integrity:**

Your word is your bond. People trust you because you are honest and ethical in your dealings.

Integrity is an indispensable quality that defines one's character and distinguishes them in various spheres of life. When you stand by your principles with unwavering integrity, you not only uphold your own values, but also earn the trust and respect of those around you. This steadfast commitment to honesty and ethical behavior establishes a solid foundation for meaningful relationships and successful endeavors.

In personal interactions, integrity forms the cornerstone of trust. When others know that your word is your bond, they feel secure in their dealings with you, knowing that you will consistently act with honesty and fairness. This fosters deep and lasting connections, as people are naturally drawn to those they can rely on and confide in.

In professional settings, unwavering integrity sets a standard of excellence. By consistently adhering to ethical practices, you inspire confidence in your abilities and create a positive reputation that precedes you. Whether in business, leadership, or any collaborative environment, integrity paves the way for successful partnerships and accomplishments.

In essence, standing by one's principles with unwavering integrity is not only a personal commitment, but also a powerful force that shapes one's impact on the world. It is a testament to strength of character and a guiding light in interactions, guiding individuals towards authenticity, trust, and the fulfillment of their highest potential.

- **Bounce back from adversity with unwavering resilience:**

Life throws punches, but you rise above them, stronger and more determined than before. Every individual encounters challenges, yet it is our response to these trials that defines our character and strength. In the face of adversity, one can harness the power of resilience to not only endure, but to grow and flourish. It is during these testing times that we discover the depths of our inner fortitude and the tenacity of the human spirit. Embracing setbacks as opportunities for growth, you transcend the limitations of the moment and emerge victorious, with newfound wisdom and a heightened sense of empowerment. Life's obstacles transform into stepping stones, propelling you towards a future filled with strength, resilience, and unwavering determination.

- **Connect with others through genuine empathy:**

You can understand and share the feelings of others, fostering strong and supportive relationships. Understanding and empathizing with others is a crucial aspect of building meaningful connections. When you are able to genuinely connect with others through empathy, you create a supportive environment that encourages open communication and trust. This not only strengthens existing relationships but also lays the foundation for new and enriching connections. Genuine empathy allows for deeper understanding and the ability to provide the necessary support and comfort to those around you.

This chapter is your roadmap to unlocking the wellspring of inner strength you possess. We'll embrace the unique characteristics that make you who you are and empower you to step into your power as someone who contributes meaningfully to the world around you. Are you ready to build the pillars of a man of value? Let's begin.

CHAPTER THREE

BUILDING CONFIDENCE AND SELF-ASSURANCE

Have you ever noticed how some people just seem to light up a room? That magnetic quality that undeniably draws, often comes from confidence. But building unshakeable self-belief can feel like a daunting task. Here's the good news: we'll tackle the challenges head-on, identify the obstacles holding you back, and equip you with powerful tools to cultivate genuine confidence.

This chapter will be your guide to developing a positive inner voice that empowers you, not belittles you. We'll explore strategies to challenge negative self-talk and replace it with affirmations that build you up. You'll learn techniques for facing your fears head-on, whether it's public speaking, asking for a raise, or simply striking up a conversation with someone new. As you confront these fears and emerge stronger on the other side, your self-assurance will grow organically. Imagine leaving self-doubt in the dust and embracing a newfound sense of self-assurance. Get ready to unleash your full potential and radiate confidence that comes from a place of authenticity and self-worth. This kind of confidence isn't about arrogance or boasting; it's about believing in yourself and your abilities and knowing that you have the power to achieve your goals.

Have you ever encountered someone who effortlessly commands attention, someone who seems to radiate an undeniable magnetism? The secret weapon behind this captivating presence is often confidence. But for many men, building unshakeable self-belief feels like scaling a mountain – a daunting and seemingly insurmountable task.

This chapter is your roadmap to conquering that peak. We'll confront the challenges head-on, identify the obstacles that hold you back from radiating confidence, and equip you with powerful tools to cultivate genuine self-belief.

Silencing the Inner Critic: Taming the Negative Voice

The journey to confidence starts with an honest look inward. Often, our greatest adversary resides within – the voice of self-doubt, the relentless critic whispering negativity in our ear. This chapter will be your guide to silencing that inner critic. We'll explore strategies to identify and challenge negative self-talk, replacing it with empowering affirmations that build you up, not tear you down.

Understanding Negative Thoughts: Negative thoughts often arise from deep-seated beliefs and assumptions about ourselves and the world around us. These thoughts can manifest as self-criticism, doubt, and fear, undermining our confidence and well-being. However, it's essential to recognize that negative thoughts are not necessarily reflective of reality — they are often distorted interpretations of our experiences.

The Practice of Reframing: Reframing involves consciously challenging and restructuring negative thoughts to create more positive and empowering interpretations. This practice requires mindfulness and self-awareness, as well as a willingness to question the accuracy of our automatic assumptions.

Practical Solutions:

- **Identify Negative Thought Patterns:**

Start by becoming aware of recurring negative thought patterns. Notice when your inner critic is most active and the specific triggers that provoke negative self-talk.

- **Challenge Negative Thoughts:**

When negative thoughts arise, challenge their validity by asking yourself questions such as:

- *Is this thought based on facts or assumptions?*
- *What evidence do I have to support or refute this thought?*
- *How would I respond if a friend expressed this same thought?*

- **Reframe with Empowering Language:**

Once you've identified and challenged negative thoughts, reframe them using positive and empowering language.

For example:

Instead of *"I'm not good enough,"* reframe to *"I am capable and deserving of success."*

Instead of *"I'll never be able to do this,"* reframe to *"I am learning and growing with each challenge."*

- ***Practice Gratitude and Perspective-Taking:***

Cultivate gratitude for your strengths, accomplishments, and the positive aspects of your life. Additionally, practice perspective-taking by considering alternative interpretations of challenging situations and recognizing the lessons and opportunities they present.

- *Create Affirmations:* Develop affirmations that counteract negative self-talk and reinforce positive beliefs about yourself. Repeat these affirmations regularly to strengthen your self-esteem and confidence.

- **Facing Your Fears: Transforming Anxiety into Action**

Fear, in all its forms, can be a significant roadblock on the path to confidence. Whether it's the paralyzing fear of public speaking, the anxiety of asking for a promotion, or the simple apprehension of approaching someone new, these fears can hold you back from reaching your full potential.

Here, you'll discover techniques for facing your fears head-on. We'll equip you with the tools to transform anxiety into action, empowering you to conquer your fears and emerge stronger on the other side. With each hurdle overcome, your self-assurance will grow organically, fueled by the knowledge that you can handle whatever life throws your way.

7. Practical Solutions for Transforming Anxiety into Action:

- **Identify Your Fears:**

Take time to identify and acknowledge the specific fears or anxieties that are holding you back. Write them down and be as specific as possible about what triggers these feelings.

- **Break It Down:**

Break down your fears into smaller, more manageable tasks or steps. This makes them feel less overwhelming and more achievable.

Create a list of action steps that you can take to confront each fear gradually.

- **Practice Relaxation Techniques:**

Incorporate relaxation techniques such as deep breathing, meditation, or progressive muscle relaxation into your daily routine.

These techniques can help calm your mind and body, making it easier to face your fears with a clear and focused mindset.

- **Challenge Negative Thoughts:**

Challenge negative thoughts and beliefs that contribute to your anxiety. Ask yourself if there is evidence to support these thoughts, and consider alternative, more realistic perspectives.

Replace negative self-talk with positive affirmations and reminders of your strengths and capabilities.

- **Set Realistic Goals:**

Set realistic and achievable goals for yourself related to confronting your fears. Break these goals down into smaller steps and celebrate your progress along the way.

Remember that progress is more important than perfection, and every step forward is a victory.

- **Take Small Steps:**

Start by facing your fears in small, manageable doses. Gradually increase the intensity or exposure as you become more comfortable.

Celebrate each small victory, no matter how seemingly insignificant it may be. Every step forward is progress.

- **Seek Support:**

Reach out to friends, family, or a therapist for support and encouragement. Talking about your fears with others can help alleviate their power and provide valuable perspective and guidance.

"Confidence: A Journey, Not a Destination"

Imagine leaving self-doubt in the dust and embracing a newfound sense of self-assurance. This chapter will empower you to do just that. Here, you'll discover the difference between genuine confidence and arrogance. We'll guide you towards a confidence rooted in self-worth and a belief in your own abilities. This is about recognizing your potential and knowing that you have the power to achieve your goals.

Building confidence is a journey, not a destination. This chapter provides the compass and the tools you need to navigate that journey. Get ready to unleash your full potential and radiate confidence that comes from a place of authenticity and self-worth. The world awaits the man you were meant to be – the confident, self-assured alpha you've always had within you.

CHAPTER FOUR

CULTIVATING LEADERSHIP SKILLS

Leadership. The word often conjures images of CEOs barking orders from corner offices or charismatic politicians delivering fiery speeches. But the truth is, leadership is a far more nuanced and accessible skill than you might think. It's not about titles or positions; it's a powerful ability that anyone can develop.

This chapter dives deep into the secrets of effective leadership, empowering you to make a positive impact in all areas of your life. Forget the outdated image of the lone leader at the front, barking orders and demanding blind obedience. Instead, we'll explore leadership as a collaborative process. It's about fostering a sense of shared purpose, where everyone feels valued, respected, and empowered to contribute their unique talents and perspectives.

The Ripple Effect: Inspiring Others to Greatness

An effective leader isn't just someone who gets things done; they're someone who inspires and motivates others to achieve their full potential. Imagine the impact you can have when you create an environment where everyone feels valued and supported. This positive energy creates a ripple effect, leading to a more successful and collaborative environment for everyone involved.

- **Leadership in Action: Beyond the Boardroom**

The beauty of leadership is its versatility. It can be exercised in countless ways, big and small. Whether you're leading a team project at work, mentoring a younger colleague, or simply taking initiative within your friend group, the power of leadership resides within you.

This chapter will be your guide to discovering your unique leadership style. We'll explore different leadership models and equip you with the tools to navigate various situations effectively. You'll learn how to:

- **Clearly communicate your vision:**

A shared vision is the foundation of any successful team. But simply stating a goal isn't enough. Effective leaders paint a vivid picture of what success looks like, inspiring and motivating others to buy into the cause. This involves clearly articulating the team's purpose, outlining the steps to achieve it, and emphasizing the positive impact their contribution will have. By communicating the "why" behind the "what," you'll ignite a fire within your team members, fostering a sense of ownership and commitment to the shared vision.

- **Delegate effectively:**

Leaders empower others, not overburden them. Delegation is a powerful tool that allows you to leverage the strengths of your team members and maximize overall productivity. However, ineffective delegation can be demotivating and lead to confusion or missed deadlines. This chapter will equip you with a proven delegation framework. You'll learn how to assess tasks, identify the right person for the job based on their skills and experience, and clearly communicate expectations. Additionally, we'll explore strategies for providing ongoing support and ensuring your team members have the resources they need to succeed. By delegating effectively, you'll free up your time to focus on strategic initiatives while fostering a sense of ownership and accountability within your team.

Motivate and inspire: People are drawn to leaders who ignite their passion and inspire them to achieve great things. But how do you cultivate that kind of motivational energy? Here are some key strategies:

- **Believing in your team:**

The first step to inspiring others is believing in their potential. When you genuinely believe in your team members' abilities, they pick up on that confidence and are more likely to believe in themselves. This creates a positive feedback loop, where trust and confidence fuel motivation and achievement

Creating a culture of recognition and appreciation:

People crave recognition for their efforts. A leader who acknowledges and celebrates accomplishments, big and small, fosters a sense of value and motivates team members to go the extra mile. Simple gestures like a public acknowledgment, a personal thank you, or a reward program can make a world of difference.

- **Framing challenges as opportunities:**

Challenges are inevitable in any endeavor. But a skilled leader can transform them into opportunities for growth and learning. By framing challenges in a positive light, emphasizing the potential for development and the value of overcoming obstacles, you can motivate your team to approach difficulties with a determined and resourceful mindset.

- *Leading by example:*

Actions speak louder than words. As a leader, you set the tone for your team. If you approach your work with passion, dedication, and a positive attitude, it will be contagious. Your enthusiasm and commitment will inspire your team members to embrace the same approach.

- **Becoming a Catalyst for Change**

By honing your leadership skills, you'll find yourself leaving a positive influence wherever you go. You won't dictate orders, but inspire and empower others to reach their full potential. This chapter equips you to become a catalyst for positive change, creating a more collaborative and successful environment for everyone around you.

"Leadership is a journey, not a destination."

Practical Solution: Assessing Tasks, Identifying the Right Person, and Communicating Expectations

- **Assess Tasks:**

Begin by clearly defining the tasks or projects that need to be completed. Break down each task into specific objectives, deadlines, and required resources.

Consider the complexity, urgency, and importance of each task to prioritize them effectively.

Determine the skills, knowledge, and experience needed to successfully complete each task.

- **Identify the Right Person for the Job:**

Assess the skills, experience, and strengths of your team members to match them with the tasks that align with their abilities.

Consider factors such as expertise, past performance, and willingness to take on new challenges.

Look beyond job titles and formal qualifications to identify individuals who have the potential to excel in specific tasks based on their unique talents and interests.

- **Communicate Expectations Clearly:**

Clearly communicate the objectives, requirements, and expectations for each task to the person assigned to it.

Provide context and background information to help them understand the importance and relevance of the task within the broader goals of the project or organization.

Set clear and realistic deadlines, milestones, and performance standards to guide their work and measure progress.

Encourage open communication and feedback to ensure that expectations are understood and aligned.

- **Provide Support and Resources:**

Offer support, guidance, and resources to help the person assigned to the task succeed. This may include access to training, tools, and information.

Be available to answer questions, address concerns, and provide clarification as needed throughout the duration of the task.

Foster a supportive and collaborative environment where team members feel comfortable seeking assistance and sharing ideas.

- **Monitor Progress and Provide Feedback:**

Regularly monitor the progress of the task and provide feedback on performance. Recognize achievements and offer constructive feedback to address areas for improvement.

Encourage accountability and ownership by empowering team members to take responsibility for their work and outcomes.

Adjust expectations and resources as needed based on changing circumstances or feedback from the person assigned to the task.

By following these practical steps, you can effectively assess tasks, identify the right person for the job, and clearly communicate expectations to ensure successful outcomes and maximize the potential of your team.

CHAPTER FIVE

Mastering Communication and Influence

They say talk is cheap, but effective communication is priceless. In today's world, the ability to articulate your thoughts, ideas, and desires clearly and persuasively is a critical skill. This chapter equips you with the tools to become a master communicator, someone who can effortlessly connect with others and achieve their goals through the power of words.

- **Beyond Words: The Power of Connection**

Communication goes far beyond simply stringing words together. It's about fostering genuine connection with others. This chapter delves into the nuances of effective communication, exploring not just what you say, but how you say it. *We'll explore the art of:*

- **Active listening:**

Effective communication is a two-way street. Truly listening to others, not just waiting for your turn to speak, is paramount. This chapter equips you with active listening skills, allowing you to grasp the full context of what's being said, understand the speaker's underlying emotions, and respond thoughtfully.

Clear and concise language:

Avoid jargon and ambiguity. Clearly articulate your thoughts and ideas in a way that is easy for your audience to understand.

- *Avoiding Jargon:* Jargon refers to specialized terminology or language that is specific to a particular field or group. While jargon may be familiar to those within the field, it can be confusing or alienating to those outside of it. When communicating with a diverse audience, it's important to use language that is universally understood and accessible to all.

- *Eliminating Ambiguity:* Ambiguity occurs when language is unclear or open to multiple interpretations. This can lead to confusion and misunderstandings. To eliminate ambiguity, strive to be as specific and precise as possible in your communication. Clearly articulate your thoughts and ideas, providing sufficient context and detail to ensure clarity.

- *Articulating Thoughts and Ideas Clearly:* Clear communication involves expressing your thoughts and ideas in a straightforward and understandable manner. This requires organizing your thoughts logically, using simple and direct language, and structuring your communication in a way that flows naturally. Avoid unnecessary complexity or verbosity, as this can hinder comprehension.

- *Considering Your Audience:* When communicating, consider the needs and preferences of your audience. Tailor your language and messaging to resonate with them, taking into account their level of expertise, background knowledge, and communication style. By understanding your audience and speaking their language, you can ensure that your message is received and understood effectively.

The Power of Persuasion: Logic, Not Manipulation

Persuasion is a powerful tool, but it shouldn't be confused with manipulation. This chapter teaches you how to craft compelling arguments that resonate with your audience, using logic and reason to win them over. *You'll learn how to:*

- **Tailor your message to your audience:**

Understanding your audience's needs, values, and perspectives is crucial for crafting a persuasive message. What resonates with one person might fall flat with another. By tailoring your communication style and content to the specific audience, you significantly increase the impact of your words.

- **Frame your message effectively:**

How you present your message can be just as important as the message itself. This chapter explores the power of framing, teaching you how to position your ideas in a way that resonates with your audience and compels them to take action.

To frame your message effectively, consider the following practical and effective solution:

- **Identify Your Objective:** Clearly define the purpose of your message and what you hope to achieve by communicating. Whether you're informing, persuading, or seeking action, having a clear objective will guide the framing of your message.

- **Focus on Benefits:** Highlight the benefits or value proposition of your message to the audience. Clearly articulate how they will benefit from taking the desired action or engaging with your message, addressing their needs, concerns, and aspirations.

- **Provide Clear Call to Action:** Clearly state what action you want your audience to take as a result of your message. Whether it's making a purchase, signing up for a newsletter, or attending an event, provide clear instructions on how they can take the next step.

Beyond Words: The Unspoken Language of Body Language

Communication isn't just about what you say; it's also about how you say it nonverbally. Your body language – posture, facial expressions, eye contact – can significantly impact how your message is received. This chapter equips you with the tools to:

- **Project confidence:**

Strong, confident body language speaks volumes. You'll learn techniques for maintaining good posture, making appropriate eye contact, and using gestures that enhance your message without appearing distracting.

To project confidence effectively, consider the following practical solutions:

- **Set Realistic Goals:**

Set achievable goals that align with your skills and abilities.
Break larger goals into smaller, manageable tasks to build momentum and confidence.

- **Prepare Thoroughly:**

Thoroughly prepare for any task, presentation, or interaction.
Research, plan, and practice until you feel comfortable and confident in your abilities.

- **3. Maintain Good Posture:**

Stand tall, with your shoulders back and your head held high.
Good posture not only conveys confidence to others but also helps you feel more confident yourself.

- **4. Use Assertive Body Language:**

Use open and expansive body language to convey confidence and authority. Make eye contact, use hand gestures purposefully, and avoid fidgeting or slouching.

- **5. Speak Clearly and Assertively:**

Speak clearly and confidently, with a strong and steady voice.
Use assertive language, avoiding hesitations, qualifiers, or apologies.

Read and respond to nonverbal cues:

Just as your body language can influence others, so can theirs. This chapter teaches you how to read nonverbal cues, allowing you to better understand the true meaning behind someone's words and tailor your communication accordingly.

To effectively read and respond to nonverbal cues, consider the following practical solutions:

- **Observe Body Language:**Pay close attention to the other person's body language, including facial expressions, gestures, posture, and eye contact. These cues can provide valuable insights into their thoughts, feelings, and intentions.

- **Stay Attentive and Present:** Be fully present and attentive during interactions, focusing on both verbal and nonverbal cues. Avoid distractions and actively listen to the other person while also observing their nonverbal behavior.

- **Be Empathetic:** Put yourself in the other person's shoes and try to empathize with their emotions and perspective. Consider how they might be feeling based on their body language and adjust your response accordingly.

- **Seek Clarification:**If you're unsure about the meaning behind someone's nonverbal cues, don't hesitate to seek clarification. Ask open-ended questions or paraphrase what you've observed to confirm your understanding and show that you're attentive to their cues.

25

The Power of Influence: A Force for Good

Effective communication is a superpower. By mastering this skill, you'll not only achieve your own goals but also leave a lasting positive impression on everyone you meet.

This chapter provides you with the roadmap and tools you need to embark on that journey. Get ready to transform yourself into a master communicator, someone whose words carry weight and whose presence commands respect.

CHAPTER SIX

HONING EMOTIONAL INTELLIGENCE

They say some of the most important battles we face are fought not on external battlefields, but within the confines of our own minds. This chapter delves into the realm of emotional intelligence (EQ), a potent tool for navigating the complexities of human interaction and emerging victorious in the war against self-destructive emotions.

Understanding Your Emotional Landscape: The Power of Self-Awareness

Imagine possessing the ability to identify your emotions as they arise, not be ruled by their overwhelming force. This chapter equips you with strategies for recognizing your emotions and the situations that trigger them. By gaining self-awareness, you'll be able to:

Name your emotions:

The first step to managing your emotions effectively is acknowledging them. This chapter provides a framework for identifying your emotional state, allowing you to move beyond simply feeling "bad" to recognizing specific emotions like anger, frustration, or sadness. By labeling your emotions, you detach from them slightly, gaining a sense of control over their influence.

Identify your emotional triggers: *Certain situations or behaviors can act as emotional triggers, hijacking your emotions and leading to impulsive reactions. But how to do that?*

- **Keep a Journal:**

  Start a journal to track your emotions and the situations that trigger them.

  Whenever you experience a strong emotional reaction, take note of the circumstances, people involved, and your thoughts and feelings at the time.

  Review your journal regularly to identify patterns and common themes among your emotional triggers.

- **Practice Mindfulness:**

  Cultivate mindfulness through practices such as meditation, deep breathing, or body scans.

  When you notice yourself experiencing strong emotions, take a moment to pause and observe them without judgment.

  Notice any physical sensations, thoughts, or behaviors associated with the emotion, and explore them with curiosity and compassion.

- **Reflect on Past Experiences:**

Reflect on past experiences that have triggered strong emotional reactions in you.

Consider how these experiences may have shaped your current emotional triggers and patterns.

Identify any unresolved issues or underlying beliefs that may be contributing to your emotional responses.

Taking Control: Effective Emotional Management

Self-awareness is just the first step. This chapter delves into strategies for managing your emotions effectively, preventing them from derailing your progress. *You'll learn how to:*

Challenge negative self-talk:

Our inner critic can be a relentless voice, fueling self-doubt and negativity. This is going to help you with tools to identify and challenge these negative thought patterns, replacing them with empowering affirmations that foster self-confidence and emotional resilience. How?

- **Cognitive Restructuring:**

Cognitive restructuring is a therapeutic technique used in cognitive-behavioral therapy (CBT) to challenge and change negative thought patterns.

Identify and examine the evidence supporting negative self-talk. Ask yourself questions such as:

Is there any evidence to support this negative thought?

What evidence exists to contradict this thought?

What would I say to a friend who had this thought?

Replace negative thoughts with more realistic and balanced interpretations. Reframe negative self-talk into statements that are compassionate, realistic, and empowering.

- **Thought Records:**

Thought records are a cognitive-behavioral tool used to track and challenge negative thoughts systematically.

Keep a thought record journal where you write down negative thoughts as they arise, along with the situation that triggered them.

Identify the cognitive distortions present in the negative thought, such as black-and-white thinking, catastrophizing, or personalization.

Challenge the negative thought by examining the evidence for and against it, as well as considering alternative perspectives.

- **Develop healthy coping mechanisms:**

Everyone experiences difficult emotions. The key is having healthy coping mechanisms to deal with them constructively. This chapter explores various techniques such as exercise, mindfulness practices, or journaling, allowing you to choose outlets that effectively manage your emotional state.

Beyond Yourself: The Art of Empathy

"Emotional intelligence isn't just about self-management; it's about understanding and empathizing with the emotions of others."

- **See the world through another's eyes:**

Imagine stepping into another person's shoes and experiencing the world from their perspective. This ability to cultivate empathy fosters deeper connections with others, allowing you to build stronger relationships and navigate conflict more effectively. By understanding the emotions behind someone's behavior, you can respond with compassion and understanding, fostering a more positive outcome.

- **Active listening for the emotional undercurrent:**

Effective communication goes beyond simply hearing words. This chapter trains you to listen actively, not just for the content of what is being said, but also for the underlying emotional tone. By picking up on nonverbal cues and emotional nuances, you can gain a deeper understanding of the person behind the words.

- ## The Benefits of High EQ: A Life Less Chaotic

By cultivating your emotional intelligence, you'll say goodbye to the constant emotional turmoil that can hinder your progress. This newfound self-awareness and ability to manage your emotions effectively will empower you to:

- **Make clear-headed decisions:**

Emotions can cloud judgment. By gaining control over your emotional state, you'll be able to approach situations with a clear mind, allowing you to make sound decisions based on logic and reason rather than impulsive reactions.

- **Navigate conflict with grace:**

Disagreements are inevitable. However, with high EQ, you'll be equipped to navigate conflict with grace and understanding. By effectively communicating your own emotions and empathizing with the other person's perspective, you can find solutions that work for everyone involved.

- **Build stronger relationships:**

People crave connection. By fostering empathy and understanding, you'll build stronger, more meaningful relationships in all aspects of your life.

Emotional intelligence is a skill that can be developed and honed over time. Get ready to transform yourself into a master of your inner world, someone who can navigate the complexities of human emotions with grace, empathy, and self-control. As you cultivate your EQ, you'll not only achieve your goals but also foster a more positive and fulfilling life for yourself and those around you.

Setting Goals and Achieving Success

Forget about stumbling into success. This chapter is going to hlep you to become the architect of your own achievements. We'll move beyond vague desires and guide you in crafting a powerful vision for the future you want to create. This vision will serve as your guiding light, a constant source of motivation and focus, reminding you of what truly matters and propelling you forward on your journey.

From Wishful Thinking to Powerful Vision: Charting Your Course

Many people wander through life with a laundry list of unfulfilled desires. This chapter challenges you to move beyond those fleeting wishes and craft a clear, compelling vision for your ideal future. We'll explore strategies for:

- **Identifying your core values:**

Your values are the fundamental principles that guide your life. Understanding your core values allows you to create a vision that is aligned with who you are at your deepest level. This ensures your goals are not just about achieving external validation, but about creating a life that feels meaningful and fulfilling to you.

- **Envisioning your ideal future:**

Close your eyes and take a moment to truly imagine your ideal life. What does success look like for you? What kind of person do you want to be? Where are you? Who are you surrounded by? By vividly describing your ideal future in detail, you create a powerful image that will serve as your guiding star.

Breaking Down Walls: Transforming Dreams into Actionable Steps

Grand visions are inspiring, but they can also feel overwhelming. This chapter dives into the art of strategic planning, transforming your big dreams into a practical roadmap. We'll explore methods for:

Setting SMART goals:

SMART is an acronym for Specific, Measurable, Achievable, Relevant, and Time-bound. Setting goals according to this framework ensures they are clear, well-defined, and attainable within a specific timeframe. This chapter equips you to craft SMART goals that are stepping stones towards your ultimate vision.

To set SMART goals effectively, consider the following practical solutions:

- **Specific**:

Clearly define the objective of your goal. Be specific about what you want to accomplish, why it's important, and what steps are involved.

Ask yourself questions such as: What exactly do I want to achieve? What is the desired outcome? Who is involved? Where will it take place?

Example: Instead of setting a vague goal like "exercise more," make it specific by saying "I will go for a 30-minute walk five days a week."

- **Measurable**:

Identify measurable criteria that will indicate progress and success toward your goal. Choose metrics or indicators that allow you to track your performance and determine if you're on track.

Ask yourself questions such as: How will I measure progress? How will I know when the goal is accomplished?

Example: Instead of saying "lose weight," make it measurable by saying "I will lose 10 pounds in three months."

- **Achievable**:

Ensure that your goal is realistic and attainable given your resources, capabilities, and constraints. Set goals that stretch you but are within reach with effort and commitment.

Ask yourself questions such as: Is this goal achievable given my current circumstances? Do I have the necessary skills, knowledge, and resources to achieve it?

Example: Instead of aiming to run a marathon next month with no prior training, set a more achievable goal like running a 5k race in three months after gradually increasing your distance.

- **Relevant**:

Make sure your goal is relevant and aligned with your values, priorities, and long-term objectives. Ensure that it matters to you and contributes to your overall vision or purpose.

Ask yourself questions such as: Is this goal relevant to my personal or professional growth? Does it align with my values and priorities?

Example: Instead of setting a goal to learn a new language when it's not relevant to your career or interests, focus on a goal that directly impacts your personal or professional development.

- **Time-bound:**

Set a specific timeframe or deadline for achieving your goal. Having a deadline creates a sense of urgency and helps you stay focused and motivated.

Ask yourself questions such as: When do I want to achieve this goal? What is the deadline or timeframe for completion?

Example: Instead of having a vague goal to "start a business someday," set a time-bound goal like "I will launch my online store by the end of the year."

By applying these practical solutions and ensuring that your goals are Specific, Measurable, Achievable, Relevant, and Time-bound, you increase the likelihood of success and empower yourself to turn your aspirations into tangible achievements.

Creating action plans:

Even the most meticulously crafted goals remain just wishes without a plan to achieve them. Creating actionable steps, breaking down your goals into smaller, manageable tasks. By creating a clear roadmap with defined milestones, you'll feel empowered and equipped to take action, one step at a time.

From Overwhelm to Progress: Prioritization and Time Management

With a clear vision and actionable steps, you might be tempted to tackle everything at once. However, this can lead to feeling overwhelmed and ultimately hinder your progress.

- **Prioritization techniques:**

Not all tasks are created equal. This chapter explores prioritization frameworks that allow you to identify the most important tasks and focus your energy accordingly. By prioritizing effectively, you'll ensure you're working on the tasks that will have the most significant impact on achieving your goals.

The Journey of Achievement: Embracing Setbacks and Celebrating Milestones

The road to success is rarely linear. There will be setbacks and challenges along the way.

- **Develop resilience:**

Setbacks are inevitable. The key is to learn from them, adapt your approach, and bounce back stronger. Setbacks are inevitable on life's path, just like bumps on a long road trip. But resilience is the fuel that gets us back behind the wheel. It's about understanding that these setbacks are temporary detours, not dead ends. By developing resilience, we can learn from our stumbles, dust ourselves off, and keep moving forward with a stronger sense of purpose and direction. Resilience isn't just about bouncing back from challenges, it's about growing from them. Each setback holds valuable lessons that can make us stronger, more adaptable, and better equipped to handle whatever comes our way. By embracing a growth mindset, we can view setbacks as opportunities to learn and refine our approach. With resilience, we can navigate the twists and turns of life's journey with greater confidence and optimism.

- **Celebrate milestones:**

Taking the time to acknowledge your accomplishments, big and small, is crucial for staying motivated. Don't just plow ahead from one goalpost to the next! Take time to celebrate milestones, big and small. These moments of acknowledgement are like pats on the back for your effort, boosting your confidence and reminding you of how far you've come. Celebrating milestones isn't just about feeling good in the moment, though. It's also a strategic way to reinforce the positive behaviors that got you there. By taking a moment to acknowledge your achievements, big or small, you solidify the mental connections between your actions and the positive outcomes they produce. This makes you more likely to repeat those behaviors in pursuit of future goals. So next time you hit a milestone, whether it's a promotion, finishing a tough workout program, or simply mastering a new skill, take a moment to savor the accomplishment. You deserve it, and this celebration will serve as a springboard to propel you forward on your journey.

From Architect to Builder: Taking Action Towards Your Dreams

Have you meticulously sketched your dream life, blueprinted your goals, and envisioned every detail of your success? That's fantastic! But dreams alone don't build a future. It's time to trade your drafting tools for a hammer and nails. "From Architect to Builder" is your call to action. It's about transforming your aspirations from paper fantasies into a tangible reality. This is where the exciting, and sometimes messy, process of construction begins.

Imagine your dreams not just as a finished masterpiece, but as a building under construction. You've poured over the blueprints, meticulously planned every detail, and now it's time to break ground. This is where the rubber meets the road, where the thrill of creation mixes with the grit of hard work. Let's take those blueprints and translate them into actionable steps, turning your dreams from a vision board into the foundation of your remarkable life. Brick by brick, you'll assemble the pieces of your dream, facing challenges head-on and emerging stronger with each hurdle overcome.

By wielding the powerful tools of goal setting and strategic planning, you'll transform from a dreamer into an architect of your own destiny. This chapter empowers you to take control of your life, turn your aspirations into tangible realities, and experience the immense satisfaction of achieving your goals.

Get ready to embark on the journey of a lifetime.

CHAPTER EIGHT

STRENGTHENING RELATIONSHIPS AND CONNECTIONS

Strengthening Relationships and Connections: Building Bridges for a Fulfilling Life

Strong relationships are the cornerstones of a happy and healthy life. They provide us with love, support, a sense of belonging, and a source of joy. They are also essential for our emotional and mental well-being. Studies have shown that strong social connections can boost our immune system, reduce stress levels, and even help us live longer. Yet, in our fast-paced world, it's easy to let busyness crowd out meaningful connection. This chapter explores the art of strengthening relationships and connections, helping you build bridges that enrich your life and create a support system that will see you through life's challenges.

The Pillars of Strong Relationships

- **Quality Time:**

In our fast-paced world, it's easy to let busyness crowd out meaningful connection. Devote quality time to the people who matter. This could be a dedicated evening with a loved one, a phone call with a distant friend, or simply putting away your devices during meals to engage in conversation. Quality time is about being fully present and engaged with the other person. Give them your undivided attention, listen actively, and savor the moments of connection.

- **Effective Communication:**

Open and honest communication is the bedrock of trust in any relationship. Actively listen to understand, express your feelings clearly, and be willing to compromise. Effective communication is a two-way street. It involves both listening attentively to what the other person is saying and expressing your own thoughts and feelings clearly and honestly. When we can communicate openly and honestly with each other, we build trust and intimacy in our relationships.

- **Empathy and Respect:**

Step into the shoes of your loved ones and try to see things from their perspective. Show genuine care for their feelings and experiences. Respect their opinions and boundaries, even when they differ from your own. Empathy and respect are the cornerstones of compassion. By putting ourselves in other people's shoes and showing respect for their thoughts and feelings, we can build stronger, more meaningful relationships.

- **Positive Regard:**

Acknowledge and appreciate the good qualities in the people around you. Offer sincere compliments and celebrate their successes. Positive regard fosters a sense of security and strengthens the bond. Look for opportunities to offer genuine compliments and praise. Let your loved ones know what you appreciate about them, both big and small. Positive regard helps people feel good about themselves and strengthens the relationships you share.

- **Mutual Support:**

Be there for your loved ones during challenging times. Offer a listening ear, a helping hand, or simply a shoulder to cry on. Reciprocate when they provide support for you. Mutual support is essential for building strong and lasting relationships. It means being there for each other through thick and thin, offering support and encouragement when needed. When we know that we can count on our loved ones to be there for us, we feel more secure and connected.

Building Bridges:

- **Active Interest:**

People crave genuine connection. Take an active interest in the lives of your loved ones. Ask thoughtful questions about their hobbies, dreams, and challenges. Go beyond superficial small talk and engage in conversations that reveal their passions, aspirations, and fears. Remember details they share and inquire about them later, showing that you were paying attention and care about what matters to them.

- **Shared Activities:**

Create lasting memories and strengthen your bond through shared experiences. Explore new hobbies together, volunteer for a cause you both care about, or simply enjoy a favorite activity together. Shared activities can be anything from cooking a meal together to taking a weekend getaway. The key is to find activities that you both enjoy and that allow you to connect on a deeper level.

- **Gratitude and Appreciation:**

Don't take your relationships for granted. Express your gratitude for the people in your life, both verbally and through your actions. Write a thank-you note, offer a helping hand with a chore, or simply tell them how much you appreciate their presence in your life. People often underestimate the power of expressing gratitude. Let your loved ones know how much they mean to you, both through your words and your actions.

- **Practice Forgiveness:**

Everyone makes mistakes. Learn to forgive others and move forward from conflict. Holding onto resentment only hurts the relationship. Forgiveness doesn't mean forgetting the hurt, but rather letting go of the anger and negative emotions associated with it. It allows you to heal and rebuild trust in the relationship.

- **Embrace Differences:**

Strong relationships are built on acceptance, not uniformity. Celebrate the unique qualities and perspectives that each person brings to the table. Appreciate the way your friends challenge your thinking or how your family members bring laughter and joy into your life. Look beyond your own perspective and embrace the richness that comes from diversity in experiences and backgrounds.

Conclusion: Cultivating a Garden of Connection

Strong relationships are not built overnight; they are nurtured and cultivated like a beautiful garden. By dedicating time and effort to the pillars of strong relationships – quality time, effective communication, empathy and respect, positive regard, and mutual support – we can build strong, lasting connections that enrich our lives. Remember to take an active interest in the lives of others, share experiences, express gratitude, practice forgiveness, and embrace differences.

While there will inevitably be disagreements and conflicts, these can be opportunities for growth if approached with respect and understanding. The key is to nurture connection, celebrate milestones, and offer support during challenging times. By putting these principles into practice, we can build a network of strong relationships that provide us with love, support, and a sense of belonging throughout our lives. So, get out there, connect with your loved ones, and cultivate a garden of connection that will bring you joy and fulfillment for years to come.

CHAPTER NINE

FITNESS, HEALTH, AND WELLNESS STRATEGIES

Fitness, Health, and Wellness Strategies for Men: A Science-Backed Approach

Men's health needs differ from women's due to several factors. Biologically, men tend to have higher muscle mass and lower body fat compared to women. This difference is due in part to hormonal variations, with men having higher levels of testosterone and women having higher levels of estrogen. Testosterone plays a key role in muscle growth and development, while estrogen is associated with fat storage. Additionally, men are more likely to experience certain health conditions, such as prostate cancer and heart disease. Socially, men may face different pressures and expectations that can impact their health behaviors. For example, men may be less likely to seek help for mental health concerns or prioritize preventative healthcare measures.

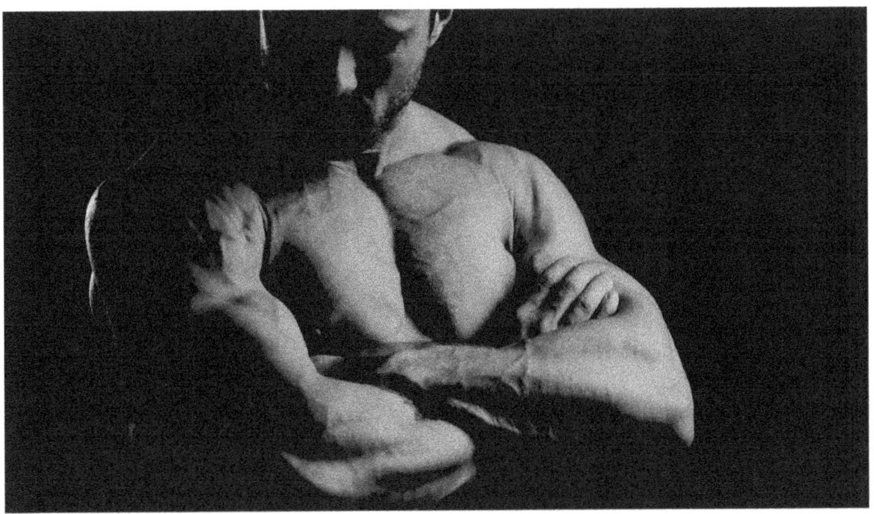

Optimizing Physical Fitness:

- **Strength Training:**

Strength training is the cornerstone of a successful fitness program for men. It builds muscle mass, which not only improves physical appearance but also boosts metabolism, increases bone density, and reduces the risk of chronic diseases like heart disease and type 2 diabetes [1, 2]. Aim for at least two to three sessions per week, focusing on compound exercises that work multiple muscle groups at once, such as squats, lunges, deadlifts, push-ups, and rows.

- **Cardiovascular Exercise:**

Regular cardiovascular exercise strengthens your heart and lungs, improves circulation, and reduces the risk of cardiovascular disease, stroke, and certain cancers [3]. Aim for at least 150 minutes of moderate-intensity aerobic activity or 75 minutes of vigorous-intensity aerobic activity per week, or a combination of both. Consider activities you enjoy, such as brisk walking, jogging, swimming, cycling, or team sports.

- **High-Intensity Interval Training (HIIT):**

HIIT involves alternating short bursts of intense exercise with periods of rest or recovery. Studies show it can be highly effective for improving cardiovascular health, burning calories, and building muscle mass, even in shorter time commitments.

Dietary Strategies for Optimal Health:

- **Balanced Macronutrients:**

Focus on a balanced diet that includes adequate protein, healthy fats, and complex carbohydrates. Protein helps with muscle building and repair, while healthy fats provide sustained energy and satiety. Complex carbohydrates, such as whole grains, fruits, and vegetables, are packed with fiber, which keeps you feeling full for longer and aids in digestion. Fiber also helps regulate blood sugar levels, reducing the risk of type 2 diabetes and promoting overall gut health. Additionally, complex carbohydrates provide a sustained source of energy to fuel your workouts and daily activities.

- **Fruits and Vegetables:**

Aim to include a variety of colorful fruits and vegetables in your diet daily. They are rich in vitamins, minerals, antioxidants, and fiber, all crucial for overall health and disease prevention.

Minimize Processed Foods:

Processed foods are often loaded with unhealthy fats, added sugars, and sodium. These can contribute to a cascade of negative health effects, including weight gain, obesity, heart disease, type 2 diabetes, and even certain cancers. Here's a breakdown of why you should minimize processed foods in your diet:

- **Unhealthy Fats:** Processed foods are frequently loaded with unhealthy fats, such as saturated fat and trans fats. These types of fats can increase LDL ("bad") cholesterol levels and raise your risk of heart disease and stroke.

- **Added Sugars:** Many processed foods are packed with added sugars, which can contribute to weight gain, obesity, and type 2 diabetes. Added sugars can also lead to a blood sugar crash, leaving you feeling tired and irritable.

- **Sodium:**Processed foods are often high in sodium, which can contribute to high blood pressure, a major risk factor for heart disease and stroke.

- **Lack of Essential Nutrients:**Processed foods are typically low in essential nutrients, such as vitamins, minerals, and fiber. These nutrients are vital for overall health and disease prevention.

By limiting processed foods and opting for whole, unprocessed options whenever possible, you can significantly improve your dietary quality and reduce your risk of chronic diseases.

Sleep for Optimal Recovery:

Prioritize Sleep: Getting enough quality sleep is critical for physical and mental health. Aim for 7-8 hours of sleep per night. Lack of sleep can impair cognitive function, increase stress hormones, and negatively impact physical performance and recovery.

Develop a Sleep Routine: Establish a consistent sleep schedule, going to bed and waking up at similar times each day, even on weekends. This helps regulate your body's natural sleep-wake cycle (circadian rhythm).

Create a Relaxing Bedtime Routine: Develop a relaxing bedtime routine that helps you wind down before sleep. This could include taking a warm bath, reading a book, or practicing relaxation techniques like deep breathing or meditation.

Mental Health and Stress Management:

Mindfulness and Meditation: Mindfulness practices like meditation can help reduce stress, improve focus, and enhance emotional well-being . There are many mindfulness apps and resources available to help you get started.

- **Social Connection:**

Strong social connections are crucial for men's mental health. Men are often socialized to be stoic and independent, but research shows that having strong social connections is essential for emotional well-being. Spending time with loved ones, such as family and friends, provides a sense of belonging, support, and companionship. Engaging in social activities can help reduce stress, loneliness, and isolation. Building a strong support network can also provide a safe space to share your feelings and concerns, and to know that you have people who care about you and will be there for you during difficult times. Strong social connections can also help to promote healthy behaviors and discourage unhealthy habits. For example, if you are surrounded by friends who are active and health-conscious, you are more likely to adopt these behaviors yourself.

- **Seek Professional Help:** If you are struggling with stress, anxiety, or depression, don't hesitate to seek professional help from a therapist or counselor.

Preventative Healthcare Measures:

- **Regular Checkups:** Schedule regular checkups with your doctor to discuss your health, monitor risk factors for chronic diseases, and get recommended screenings such as prostate cancer screenings and blood pressure checks

- **Healthy Habits:** Maintain healthy lifestyle habits such as not smoking, limiting alcohol consumption, and maintaining a healthy weight to minimize the risk of chronic diseases.

Remember: Consistency is Key

The most effective fitness, health, and wellness strategies are those that you can maintain consistently over time. Find activities you enjoy, set realistic goals, and track your progress. Celebrate your milestones and don't be discouraged by setbacks. With dedication and a commitment to a healthy lifestyle, you can achieve optimal physical and mental well-being.

Scientific References:

[1] Schoenfeld BJ, Ogborn D, Krieger JW. Effects of resistance training volume on measures of muscle hypertrophy in healthy young men. J Strength Cond Res. 2017;31(1):100-108. doi:10.1519/ JSC.0000000000001"

CHAPTER TEN

OVERCOMING CHALLENGES AND ADVERSITY

Overcoming Challenges and Adversity: Building Resilience in the Face of Difficulty

Life is an unpredictable journey, filled with both sunshine and storms. Challenges and adversity are inevitable, appearing in various forms – setbacks in our careers, strained relationships, financial difficulties, health issues, or the loss of loved ones. While these experiences can be daunting, they also present opportunities for growth and self-discovery. The key lies in developing resilience, the ability to bounce back from adversity, learn from setbacks, and emerge stronger than before.

Understanding the Impact of Challenges:

Challenges can trigger a range of emotions, including fear, anger, frustration, and sadness. These emotions are a natural response to the disruption of our expectations and comfort zones. However, dwelling on these emotions can hinder our ability to cope effectively. Acknowledging your emotions is important, but don't let them control you.

- **Building the Blocks of Resilience:**

Mindset Matters: Our mindset significantly influences how we approach challenges. A fixed mindset views setbacks as permanent limitations, while a growth mindset sees them as opportunities to learn and improve. Cultivating a growth mindset allows you to reframe challenges as stepping stones on your path to success.

- **Developing Self-Awareness:**

Understanding your strengths and weaknesses is crucial for navigating challenges effectively. Identify areas where you excel and those that require further development. This self-awareness empowers you to approach challenges with a sense of agency and focus on areas where you can make a positive impact.

- **Building a Support System:**

No one is meant to face adversity alone. Surround yourself with positive and supportive people who believe in you and your ability to overcome challenges. A strong support system can provide emotional encouragement, practical assistance, and a safe space to express your concerns.

Coping Mechanisms for Effective Response:

- **Problem-Solving Skills:**

When faced with a challenge, take a step back and assess the situation rationally. Break down the problem into smaller, more manageable steps. Explore potential solutions, considering the potential outcomes of each approach.

- **Stress Management Techniques:**

Chronic stress can significantly impede your ability to cope effectively. Develop healthy stress management techniques like mindfulness meditation, deep breathing exercises, or regular physical activity.

- **Developing Grit:**

Grit is the unwavering passion and perseverance to pursue long-term goals despite setbacks. Developing grit empowers you to stay committed to your goals even when the going gets tough.

- **Finding Meaning in Challenges:**

Sometimes, challenges can be reframed as opportunities for growth and self-discovery. Ask yourself what you can learn from this experience. How can you use this setback to become a stronger, more resilient person?

Moving Forward with Confidence:

Celebrate Milestones: Acknowledge and celebrate your progress, no matter how small. Taking the time to acknowledge your achievements reinforces positive behaviors and motivates you to keep moving forward.

- **Learn from Setbacks:**

Every challenge presents an opportunity to learn and grow. Reflect on what went wrong and identify areas for improvement. Use this knowledge to inform your future actions and decision-making.

- **Maintain a Positive Outlook:**

Maintaining a positive outlook doesn't mean ignoring the challenges you face. Instead, it means holding onto the belief that you have the ability to overcome them. Focus on the things you can control and visualize yourself achieving your goals.

Remember: Overcoming challenges is a journey, not a destination. There will be setbacks along the way, but with the right mindset, coping mechanisms, and a strong support system, you can build resilience and emerge from adversity stronger and more prepared for whatever life throws your way.

CHAPTER ELEVEN

POLISHING THE DIAMOND - MASTERING PERSONALITY GROOMING

Men's grooming is more than just superficial; it's about presenting a well-cared-for version of yourself that projects confidence and self-respect. It encompasses a variety of practices that enhance your appearance, improve your hygiene, and boost your overall well-being. This chapter delves into the essential aspects of men's grooming, providing a roadmap to refine your facial features, hairstyle, and clothing choices for both formal and casual settings. By following these tips, you can elevate your everyday look and create a lasting impression.

Face

Skincare Basics: Develop a regular skincare routine that cleanses, hydrates, and protects your skin. Wash your face twice daily with a gentle cleanser suitable for your skin type. Apply a moisturizer to keep your skin hydrated and prevent dryness.Sunscreen is essential, even on cloudy days, to protect your skin from harmful UV rays. Consider incorporating a facial oil, like almond oil, into your nighttime routine for added hydration. Almond oil is a natural emollient that can help soften and soothe the skin. However, be sure to choose a light, non-comedogenic oil to avoid clogging your pores.

Shaving: Master the art of a clean shave. Here's what you'll need:

- **Sharp Razor**: A dull razor can cause irritation and nicks. Invest in a quality razor with multiple blades, and replace the cartridge regularly (typically after 5-7 shaves).

- **Shaving Cream or Gel:** Using a shaving cream or gel helps soften your beard hair and lubricate the skin, reducing friction and razor burn. Choose a product that suits your skin type, such as a hydrating formula for dry skin or a sensitive skin formula for those prone to irritation.

- **Pre-Shave Oil (Optional):** For an extra layer of protection and a closer shave, consider using a pre-shave oil. Apply a thin layer to damp skin before lathering up with shaving cream.

- **Warm Water:** Splash your face with warm water to open up your pores and soften your beard hair. This makes for a more comfortable and effective shave.

Shaving Technique

- Apply a hot towel to your face for a minute or two. This further helps soften your beard and opens your pores.
- Lather up your shaving cream or gel, ensuring you get a good coverage over your entire beard area.
- Shave with the grain first, using short, gentle strokes. Avoid applying too much pressure, and let the razor do the work.
- Rinse your face with cool water to close your pores.
- Apply a post-shave balm or lotion to soothe and hydrate your skin.
- Shaving aftercare is crucial to prevent irritation and razor bumps. Exfoliate your skin regularly, 2-3 times per week, to remove dead skin cells and prevent ingrown hairs. A gentle exfoliating scrub can help remove buildup and keep your skin smooth. You can also use a chemical exfoliant, such as those containing alpha hydroxy acids (AHAs), to gently remove dead skin cells and promote cell turnover. After exfoliating, always moisturize your skin to replenish hydration.

For a touch of definition, consider shaping your beard or mustache. A beard trimmer with various attachments allows you to create different styles and maintain clean lines. Remember to trim regularly to keep your facial hair neat and avoid a patchy appearance.

Facial Hair: Whether you prefer a clean-shaven look, a beard, or a mustache, maintain it with care. Trim regularly to keep it neat and avoid a scraggly appearance. If you're sporting a beard, invest in a beard oil to keep it conditioned and prevent itchiness.

Hair

- **Find Your Signature Style:** Choose a hairstyle that complements your face shape and hair texture. Consider low-maintenance options like short fades, crew cuts, or textured cuts with a bit more length on top. Talk to your barber about styles that suit your needs and lifestyle.

- **Hair Care:** Maintain a healthy scalp and hair with a proper hair care routine. Avoid harsh chemicals and excessive heat styling. Consider a leave-in conditioner or styling product to manage frizz or add volume. You can also explore natural hair care options like applying onion oil to nourish your scalp and hair. Onion oil is rich in sulfur, which can promote healthy hair growth. However, avoid shampooing every day, as this can strip your hair of its natural oils. If your hair gets oily, consider using a dry shampoo between washes.

- **Grooming on the Go:** Keep a travel-sized comb or brush handy to maintain your hairstyle throughout the day.

Jawline

A defined jawline is often associated with masculinity and a youthful appearance. While genetics play a significant role in jawline structure, there are steps men can take to enhance its definition and create a more chiseled look. Here's a comprehensive guide to achieving a sharper jawline:

Diet and Exercise

- **Weight Management:** Maintaining a healthy weight reduces overall facial fat, allowing your jawline to become more prominent. Focus on a balanced diet rich in fruits, vegetables, and whole grains, while limiting processed foods, sugary drinks, and unhealthy fats.

- **Facial Exercises:** While scientific evidence on the effectiveness of isolated facial exercises for jawline definition is limited, some exercises may help strengthen and tone the underlying muscles. Here are a few examples:

- **Chewing Gum:** Chewing sugar-free gum can provide a light workout for your jaw muscles.

- **Neck Flexions:** Sit upright with your back straight and shoulders relaxed. Slowly tilt your head back as far as comfortably possible, hold for a few seconds, and then return to the starting position. Repeat 10-15 times.

- **Jaw Clenches:** Clench your jaw as if chewing something tough, hold for a few seconds, and then relax. Repeat 10-15 times.

- **Cardio:** Regular cardiovascular exercise promotes overall health and helps reduce facial fat, contributing to a more defined jawline. Aim for at least 150 minutes of moderate-intensity aerobic activity or 75 minutes of vigorous-intensity aerobic activity per week.

Skincare

Collagen Production: Collagen is a protein that provides structure and elasticity to the skin. As we age, collagen production decreases, leading to sagging skin and a less defined jawline. Here are some ways to promote collagen production:

- **Retinol:** Topical application of retinol creams can stimulate collagen production and improve skin texture.
- **Vitamin C:** Vitamin C is another antioxidant that may help boost collagen production. Consider incorporating a Vitamin C serum into your skincare routine.
- **Healthy Diet:** A diet rich in fruits, vegetables, and lean protein provides the necessary building blocks for collagen synthesis.
- **Exfoliation:** Regular exfoliation removes dead skin cells and promotes cell turnover, revealing a brighter and more youthful complexion. Opt for a gentle exfoliating scrub suitable for your skin type.
- **Lifestyle Habits**
- **Hydration:** Drinking plenty of water throughout the day keeps your skin plump and hydrated, contributing to a more defined jawline. Aim for eight glasses of water daily.

- **Sleep:** Adequate sleep is crucial for overall health and skin health. When you're sleep-deprived, your body produces more cortisol, a stress hormone that can lead to increased facial fat storage. Aim for 7-8 hours of quality sleep each night.

Considerations and Alternatives

Realistic Expectations: Genetics play a major role in jawline structure. While you can enhance definition, it's important to have realistic expectations about the results you can achieve naturally.

Consulting a Dermatologist: If you're looking for more dramatic results, consider consulting a dermatologist who can discuss minimally invasive procedures like jawline fillers or Botox injections. However, these procedures come with risks and should be carefully considered before making a decision.

Formal Clothing

Formal attire exudes sophistication and professionalism, making a powerful statement in business settings and special occasions. However, looking your best in formals goes beyond just throwing on a suit. Here's a detailed guide to ensure you exude confidence and make a lasting impression while rocking formal wear:

Finding the Perfect Fit:

- **Tailoring is King:** Off-the-rack suits rarely fit perfectly. Invest in a good tailor who can adjust your suit for a flawless fit. A properly tailored suit should hug your shoulders comfortably without restricting movement. The sleeves should show a quarter-inch of shirt cuff, and the pants should drape cleanly over your shoes with a slight break (single or double depending on your style preference).

- **Dress Shirt Nuances:** A well-fitting dress shirt complements your suit and flatters your physique. The collar should rest comfortably against your neck without feeling too tight or loose. The sleeves should extend slightly beyond your jacket cuff, revealing a quarter-inch to half-inch of shirt cuff. The shirt should stay tucked in throughout the day, so choose a size that fits your waist comfortably without billowing.

Polishing Your Look

- **Shoe Selection:** Formal attire demands well-polished leather shoes. Oxfords are a timeless choice for suits, offering a sleek and sophisticated look. Derbies can also work for formal separates, providing a slightly less formal vibe. Ensure your shoes are free of scuffs and scratches. Invest in good quality shoe polish and regularly buff your shoes to maintain their shine.

- **Sock Etiquette:** Formal attire requires dress socks that reach mid-calf and coordinate with your suit trousers. Avoid novelty socks with loud patterns or colors. Opt for solid colors or subtle patterns that complement your overall look.

- **Belt Basics:** Your belt should match the color of your shoes as closely as possible. Leather belts are the preferred choice for formal wear. Choose a belt with a simple buckle design that complements the formality of your outfit.

- **Tie it Right:** A well-tied tie completes your formal ensemble. Choose a tie that complements your suit and shirt color. There are many different tie knots, with the Windsor knot being a versatile and classic option for formal occasions. Practice your tie-tying skills beforehand to ensure a clean and symmetrical knot.

Taking Care of Details

- **Pocket Square:** A pocket square adds a touch of personality and elevates your formal attire. Opt for a pocket square made from silk or cotton that complements your tie and suit. There are various pocket square folding techniques, with the presidential fold being a simple and elegant choice for formal occasions.

- **Cufflinks:** Cufflinks add a touch of sophistication and replace the functional buttons on a French-cuffed dress shirt. Choose cufflinks made from high-quality materials like silver or gold that complement your overall style.

- **Minimal Jewelry:** Formal attire calls for minimal jewelry. A simple watch and a wedding band are typically sufficient. Avoid wearing flashy jewelry or excessive rings.

- **Minimal Fragrance:** Apply a subtle amount of cologne before heading out. A strong overpowering scent can be distracting and off-putting in a formal setting.

Posture and Confidence

- **Stand Tall:** Maintain good posture throughout the event. Stand tall with your shoulders back and your head held high. Good posture not only projects confidence but also flatters your formal attire.

- **Confidence is Key:** The most important accessory is your confidence. When you feel good about yourself, it shows. Walk into the event with a confident demeanor and a smile.

By following these tips and paying attention to the finer details, you can ensure a polished and professional look that commands respect and makes a lasting impression in any formal setting. Remember, looking sharp is about more than just the clothes; it's about carrying yourself with confidence and self-assuredness.

Casual Clothing

Casual wear doesn't have to be sloppy. By focusing on fit, quality basics, and thoughtful layering, you can elevate your casual look and project a well-put-together image. Here's a detailed guide to taking care of business when it comes to casual clothing:

Fit is Everything

- **Finding Your Silhouette:** Even casual clothes should flatter your body type. Baggy clothes can make you look bigger than you are, while overly tight clothing can be uncomfortable and unflattering. Choose clothes that fit you well without being restrictive.

- **T-Shirt Talk:** A well-fitting T-shirt forms the foundation of many casual outfits. Opt for crewneck or V-neck T-shirts made from high-quality cotton that drapes comfortably over your torso. Avoid overly baggy or excessively tight T-shirts.

- **Denim Decoded:** Jeans are a staple in any man's wardrobe. Choose a style that complements your body type. Straight-leg jeans are a versatile option that works well on most body shapes. Darker washes tend to be more slimming and project a more polished look.

Elevating Your Basics

- **Invest in Quality:** You don't need a massive wardrobe, but invest in high-quality basics that will last. A few well-made T-shirts, a couple of pairs of jeans in different washes, and a few well-fitting chinos will provide a solid foundation for countless casual outfits.

- **Beyond the Basics:** Expand your casual wardrobe with versatile pieces like button-down shirts, light jackets (denim jackets, bomber jackets), and sweaters. These add variety and allow you to create different looks for various occasions.

Layering Like a Pro

- **Master the Art:** Layering is a powerful tool to add dimension and style to your casual look. Try layering a T-shirt under a button-down shirt, or a light jacket over a t-shirt and jeans. Layering also allows you to adapt to changing temperatures throughout the day.

- **Color Coordination:** Choose colors that complement each other. Neutral colors like black, white, navy, and gray form a solid base, and you can add pops of color with statement pieces like a brightly colored shirt or a patterned jacket.

Taking Care of the Details

- **Footwear Matters:** The right shoes can elevate your casual look. Sneakers are a go-to option, but choose styles that complement your overall outfit. Loafers or boots can also work well with certain casual looks.

- **Accessorize Wisely:** Accessories can add a touch of personality to your casual look. A simple watch, a leather belt, or a hat can elevate your outfit without going overboard. Keep it simple and avoid wearing too many accessories at once.

- **Hairstyle and Grooming:** Don't neglect your hairstyle and grooming when rocking casual wear. Maintain a clean and tidy hairstyle that complements your face shape. A well-groomed beard or mustache can also enhance your casual look.

Confidence is Key

- **Own Your Style:** Ultimately, the best way to look good in casual wear is to feel confident in what you're wearing. Develop your own personal style and wear clothes that make you feel good about yourself. Confidence is the most attractive accessory you can wear.

   *"**Bonus Tip:**Garment Care: Take care of your clothes! Wash them according to the instructions on the care label and fold or hang them properly to prevent wrinkles. Taking care of your clothes ensures they last longer and maintain their shape, contributing to a more polished*

look overall. "

Remember: Confidence is the ultimate accessory. When you feel good about yourself, it shows. Take pride in your appearance, and let your inner confidence shine through.

FROM ORDINARY TO EXTRAORDINARY: LESSONS FROM FIVE BOOKS ON HIGH-VALUE LIVING

THE WAY OF MEN BY JACK DONOVAN (Book 1)

The Way of Men" by Jack Donovan is a thought-provoking exploration of masculinity in the modern world. Donovan delves into the essence of manhood, arguing that at its core, masculinity is defined by strength, courage, mastery, and honor. Drawing on evolutionary psychology, anthropology, and historical examples, he posits that traditional masculine virtues are rooted in the primal instincts of survival and tribal cooperation.

Donovan argues that contemporary society has lost touch with these primal aspects of masculinity, leading to confusion and dissatisfaction among men. He suggests that men must reclaim their innate masculinity by embracing their roles as protectors, providers, and warriors. Through a combination of self-reliance, physical prowess, and loyalty to kin and tribe, men can forge bonds of brotherhood and establish their place in the world.

"The Way of Men" challenges conventional notions of masculinity and offers a compelling vision for men seeking to reconnect with their primal nature. Donovan's provocative insights and bold assertions spark introspection and debate, prompting readers to reconsider their understanding of what it means to be a man in today's society.

Man's Search for Meaning" by Viktor E (Book 2)

Man's Search for Meaning" by Viktor E. Frankl is a profound and moving exploration of the human experience in the face of suffering and adversity. Frankl, a psychiatrist and Holocaust survivor, reflects on his time in Nazi concentration camps and the profound insights he gained into the nature of human existence.

The book is divided into two parts. In the first part, Frankl describes his experiences in the concentration camps, where he endured unimaginable hardships and witnessed the depths of human cruelty. Despite the horrors of his circumstances, Frankl reflects on the power of the human spirit to find meaning and purpose even in the most desperate of situations.

In the second part of the book, Frankl introduces his theory of logotherapy, a psychotherapeutic approach based on the belief that the primary drive in human beings is the search for meaning. Drawing on his experiences in the concentration camps, Frankl argues that even in the most dire circumstances, individuals can find meaning in their lives by embracing their inherent freedom to choose their attitude in any given situation.

"Man's Search for Meaning" is a deeply philosophical and introspective work that explores fundamental questions about the nature of suffering, the pursuit of happiness, and the quest for meaning in life. Frankl's insights continue to resonate with readers around the world, offering profound wisdom and inspiration in the face of adversity.

Iron John: A Book About Men" by Robert Bly (Book 3)

Iron John: A Book About Men" by Robert Bly is a transformative exploration of masculinity and the journey of men in contemporary society. Drawing on folklore, mythology, psychology, and personal anecdotes, Bly delves into the challenges and opportunities facing men as they navigate the complexities of modern life.

The book centers around the archetype of Iron John, a figure from the Brothers Grimm fairy tale who represents wildness, masculinity, and the untamed aspects of the male psyche. Bly uses the story of Iron John as a lens through which to explore the various stages of male development, from boyhood to manhood.

Bly argues that modern society often suppresses and undermines the natural instincts and qualities of masculinity, leading to confusion and dissatisfaction among men. He calls for a return to the primal aspects of masculinity, urging men to reconnect with their inner wildness, strength, and vitality.

Through a combination of psychological insights and poetic prose, Bly invites readers to embark on a journey of self-discovery and personal growth. He explores themes such as the father-son relationship, the importance of male initiation rituals, and the need for men to embrace both their light and shadow sides.

"Iron John" challenges conventional notions of masculinity and offers a vision for men to reclaim their authentic selves and fulfill their potential. Bly's profound observations and timeless wisdom continue to resonate with readers, inspiring them to embrace their masculinity with courage, integrity, and compassion.

"Mastery" by Robert Greene (Book 4)

Mastery" by Robert Greene is a compelling examination of the path to excellence and mastery in any field. Drawing on the lives of historical figures, contemporary masters, and his own extensive research, Greene explores the principles and strategies that underlie the journey to mastery.

The book is divided into three sections: Apprenticeship, Creative-Active, and Mastery. In the Apprenticeship phase, Greene emphasizes the importance of humility, patience, and dedication as individuals embark on their journey toward mastery. He explores the role of mentors, apprenticeships, and the acquisition of fundamental skills in laying the foundation for future success.

In the Creative-Active phase, Greene delves into the process of innovation, creativity, and self-discovery. He encourages readers to experiment, take risks, and embrace failure as opportunities for growth. Greene explores the importance of intuition, intuition, and adaptability in navigating the challenges of mastery.

In the Mastery phase, Greene examines the culmination of years of dedication, practice, and perseverance. He profiles individuals who have achieved mastery in their respective fields, highlighting the common traits and strategies that have propelled them to greatness. Greene emphasizes the importance of continual learning, self-awareness, and a relentless pursuit of excellence in sustaining mastery over the long term.

"Mastery" is a thought-provoking and practical guide for anyone seeking to achieve excellence in their chosen field. Greene's insights into the nature of mastery, combined with his engaging storytelling and historical examples, make this book a valuable resource for individuals striving to unlock their full potential and become masters of their craft.

The Rational Male" by Rollo Tomassi (Book 5)

"The Rational Male" by Rollo Tomassi is a provocative exploration of intersexual dynamics and the nature of masculinity in contemporary society. Drawing on evolutionary psychology, sociology, and personal anecdotes, Tomassi challenges conventional wisdom about gender relations and offers a bold, unapologetic perspective on male-female dynamics.

The book is divided into three main sections: "Rationalization," "Relational Dynamics," and "Social Paradigms." In the first section, Tomassi discusses the concept of "The Rational Male," arguing that men must embrace a rational, pragmatic approach to understanding and navigating the complexities of modern relationships. He explores common misconceptions and delusions that men often fall victim to in their interactions with women, urging readers to adopt a more objective and realistic view of human nature.

In the second section, Tomassi delves into the dynamics of male-female relationships, examining concepts such as hypergamy, female sexual strategy, and the nature of attraction. He explores the evolutionary underpinnings of these dynamics, offering insights into why men and women behave the way they do in romantic and sexual contexts.

In the final section, Tomassi explores broader social and cultural paradigms that shape male-female relationships. He discusses topics such as feminism, gender roles, and the impact of modernity on traditional notions of masculinity and femininity. Tomassi argues that understanding these larger social forces is crucial for men seeking to navigate the challenges of modern dating and relationships.

The Rational Male" is a thought-provoking and controversial book that challenges readers to rethink their assumptions about gender and relationships. Tomassi's insights into the nature of masculinity, female psychology, and societal dynamics provoke debate and discussion, making this book a must-read for anyone interested in understanding the complexities of male-female dynamics in the modern world.